Classic Afghans

The Best of Mary Maxim®

LEISURE ARTS, INC. • Maumelle, Arkansas

Cozy Colorful Throw

INTERMEDIATE

SHOPPING LIST

Yarn (DK /Sport Weight) LIGHT 3

Mary Maxim Prism
[3.5 ounces, 290 yards
(100 grams, 265 meters) per ball]:
- ☐ Prism (A) 5 balls

Mary Maxim Ultra Mellowspun
[1.75 ounces, 174 yards
(50 grams, 160 meters) per ball]:
- ☐ Brown (B) 6 balls

Knitting Needles
- ☐ Size 7 (4.50 mm)
  or size needed for gauge

SIZE INFORMATION

Finished: 48" x 48" [122 x 122 cm]

GAUGE INFORMATION

Mitered Square = 4.5" [11.5 cm] square and a finished Block = 12" [30.5 cm] square, using **suggested** needles or any size needles which will give the correct stitch gauge.

STITCH GUIDE

ssk Slip next 2 sts knitwise, one at a time, to right needle, then insert left needle through fronts of both sts and k2tog as usual.

Note: Each Block consists of 4 Mitered Squares, joined as they are worked. The Block then has a border worked on each edge.

INSTRUCTIONS

Block: (make 16)

Using A, cast on 44 sts.

First Mitered Square:

****Row 1:*** Knit.

Row 2: (*right side*) K 20, ssk, PM, k2tog, k to end. (42 sts)

Row 3 and every alternate row: Knit.

Row 4: K to 2 sts before M, ssk, sl M, k2tog, k to end.

Repeat these last 2 rows, dec 2 sts every alternate row, until 2 sts rem.

Next Row: K2tog.

Fasten off.**

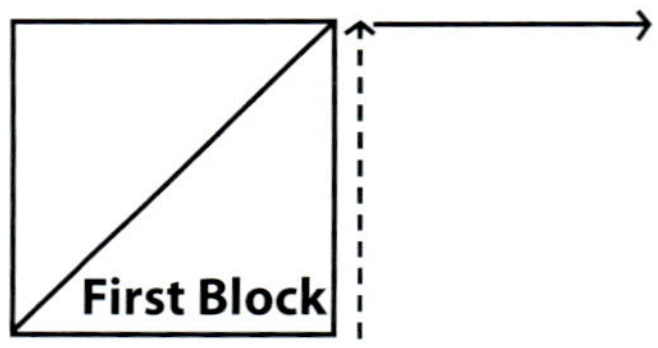

2nd Square: Hold First Square with cast on edge across top and to the right (see diagram above), with right side facing,
pick up 22 sts along right side edge of First Square (see dotted line),
then using Backwards Loop cast on method (see page 3), cast on 22 sts. (44 sts on needle)

Work as given for First Square from ** to **.

3rd Square: Hold previous squares with 2nd Square on the right, having cast on edges at top, and with right sides facing, pick up 22 sts across top of 2nd Square, cast on 22 sts as before. (44 sts)

Work as given for First Square from ** to **.

4th Square: With right sides of previous squares facing, pick up 22 sts along side of 3rd Square, pick up 22 sts along top of First Square - 44 sts.

Work as given for First Square from ** to **.

Four Mitered Squares are now joined and complete.

Short Borders: With right side of squares facing, using B, pick up and k 44 sts across one edge (22 sts per square).

Knit 10 rows. Cast off knitwise, keeping cast off smooth and even.

Repeat on opposite edge.

Long Borders: With right side of squares facing, working across one of the unworked edges, pick up and k5 sts along end of Short Border, pick up and k 44 sts across squares, pick up and k5 sts along end of other Short Border. (54 sts)

Knit 10 rows. Cast off knitwise, keeping cast off smooth and even.

Repeat on opposite edge.

Work rem 15 Blocks the same.

To Assemble: Lay Blocks out as desired, forming 4 rows of 4 Blocks and matching Long Border and Short Borders.

Sew Blocks tog neatly.

Weave in all ends securely.

Backwards Loop cast on

Put a loop on the needle; notice the direction of the movement of the yarn...

tighten it up... one st has been cast on. Continue in this manner to the given number of sts.

Uptown Throw

INTERMEDIATE

SHOPPING LIST

Yarn (Bulky Weight) BULKY 5

Mary Maxim Studio

[3.5 ounces, 160 yards

(100 grams, 146 meters) per ball]:

☐ Oil Paints 6 balls

Knitting Needle

32" (80 cm) Circular Needle

☐ Size 15(10.00 mm)

or size needed for gauge

SIZE INFORMATION

Finished: 38" x 50" [96.5 x 127 cm]

GAUGE INFORMATION

9 sts and 12 rows to 4" [10 cm] measured over pattern using **suggested** needle or any size needle which will give the correct gauge.

STITCH GUIDE

Note: Yo's DO NOT count as a stitch.

INSTRUCTIONS

Cast on 86 sts.

Knit 9 rows.

Next Row: (*wrong side*) K6, PM, *k1, yo, sl 1P; rep from * to last 6 sts, PM, k6.

Now work in pattern as follows, slipping markers on every row:

Row 1: (*right side*) K6, *k1, sl yo purlwise, k1; rep from * to last 6 sts, k6.

Row 2: K6, *yo, sl 1P, k2tog (the yo and the next st); rep from * to last 6 sts, k6.

Row 3: K6, *k2, sl yo purlwise; rep from * to last 6 sts, k6.

Row 4: K6, *k2tog (yo and the next st), yo, sl 1P; rep from * to last 6 sts, k6.

Repeat Rows 1-4 until work measures about 48" [122 cm] from cast on edge, ending after a Row 3.

Next Row: K6, *k2tog (yo and the next st), sl 1P; rep from * to last 6 sts, k6.

Knit 8 rows.

Cast off knitwise.

Sew in all ends securely.

Cables & Twists Throw

Shown on page 7.

EXPERIENCED

SHOPPING LIST

Yarn (Worsted Weight) MEDIUM 4

Mary Maxim Woodlands
[3.5 ounces, 200 yards
(100 grams, 183 meters) per ball]:

- ☐ Ecru 4 balls
- ☐ Lt Brown 4 balls
- ☐ Dk Brown 5 balls
- ☐ Grey 4 balls

Knitting Needles

- ☐ Size 8 (5.00 mm)

or size needed for gauge

SIZE INFORMATION

Finished: 48" x 60" [122 x 152.5 cm]

GAUGE INFORMATION

Center Cable = 5.75" [14.5 cm] wide,
Panel 1 = 4" [10 cm] wide,
Panel 2 = 5" [12.5 cm] wide,
Panel 3 = 4" [10 cm] wide,
Panel 4 = 3" [7.5 cm] wide and
Panel 5 = 5.25" [13 cm] wide
all using the **suggested** needles or any size needles which will give the correct gauges.

STITCH GUIDE

kf&b Increase one st by knitting into front and back of next st.

C6B Slip next 3 sts onto cable needle and hold to back of work, k3 from left-hand needle, then k3 from cable needle.

C6F Slip next 3 sts onto cable needle and hold to front of work, k3 from left-hand needle, then k3 from cable needle.

T5F Slip next 3 sts onto cable needle and hold to front of work, p2 from left-hand needle, then k3 from cable needle.

T5B Slip next 2 sts onto cable needle and hold to back of work, k3 from left-hand needle, then p2 from cable needle.

C4R Slip next st onto cable needle and hold to back of work, k3 from left-hand needle, then p1 from cable needle.

C4L Slip next 3 sts onto cable needle and hold to front of work, p1 from left-hand needle, then k3 from cable needle.

C4F Slip next 2 sts onto cable needle and hold to front of work, k2 from left-hand needle, then k2 from cable needle.

C4B Slip next 2 sts onto cable needle and hold to back of work, k2 from left-hand needle, then k2 from cable needle.

C3L Slip next st onto cable needle and hold to front of work, p2 from left-hand needle, then k1 from cable needle.

C3R Slip next 2 sts onto cable needle and hold to back of work, k1 from left-hand needle, then p2 from cable needle.

T2FP Working on wrong side, slip next st onto cable needle and hold to front of work, p1 from left-hand needle, then p1 from cable needle.

T3B Slip next st onto cable needle and hold to back of work, k2 from left-hand needle, then p1 from cable needle.

T3F Slip next 2 sts onto cable needle and hold to front of work, p1 from left-hand needle, then k2 from cable needle.

T4B Slip next 2 sts onto cable needle and hold to back of work, k2 from left-hand needle, then p2 from cable needle.

T4F Slip next 2 sts onto cable needle and hold to front of work, p2 from left-hand needle, then k2 from cable needle.

Important Note:
Panels have different number of rows, but all end with the same length.

INSTRUCTIONS

Center Panel: (worked over 44 sts)

Using Ecru, cast on 33 sts.

Knit 4 rows.

Row 1: (*right side*) K1, p1, k3, [(kf&b) twice, k3] twice, [kf&b] 3 times, [k3, (kf&b) twice] twice, k3, p1, k1. (44 sts)

Row 2: K1, p2, k2, [p3, k4] twice, p6, [k4, p3] twice, k2, p2, k1.

Row 3: K1, p1, k1, p2, [k3, p4] twice, C6B, [p4, k3] twice, p2, k1, p1, k1.

Row 4: As Row 2.

Row 5: K1, p1, k1, p2, k3, p4, [T5F, T5B] twice, p4, k3, p2, k1, p1, k1.

Row 6: K1, p2, k2, p3, k6, p6, k4, p6, k6, p3, k2, p2, k1.

Row 7: K1, p1, k1, p2, T5F, p4, [C6F, p4] twice, T5B, p2, k1, p1, k1.

Row 8: K1, p2, k4, p3, k4, [p6, k4] twice, p3, k4, p2, k1.

Row 9: K1, p1, k1, p4, [T5F, T5B] 3 times, p4, k1, p1, k1.

Row 10: K1, p2, k6, p6, [k4, p6] twice, k6, p2, k1.

Row 11: K1, p1, k1, p6, C6B, [p4, C6B] twice, p6, k1, p1, k1.

Row 12: As Row 10.

Row 13: K1, p1, k1, p4, [T5B, T5F] 3 times, p4, k1, p1, k1.

Row 14: As Row 8.

Row 15: K1, p1, k1, p4, k3, [p4, C6F] twice, p4, k3, p4, k1, p1, k1.

Row 16: As Row 8.

Row 17: As Row 9.

Row 18: As Row 10.

Row 19: As Row 11.

Row 20: As Row 10.

Row 21: As Row 13.

Row 22: As Row 8.

Row 23: K1, p1, k1, p2, T5B, p4, [C6F, p4] twice, T5F, p2, k1, p1, k1.

Row 24: As Row 6.

Row 25: K1, p1, k1, p2, k3, p4, [T5B, T5F] twice, p4, k3, p2, k1, p1, k1.

Row 26: As Row 2.

Row 27: K1, p1, k1, p2, [k3, p4] twice, C6B, [p4, k3] twice, p2, k1, p1, k1.

Row 28: As Row 2.

Row 29: K1, p1, k1, p2, [k3, p4] twice, k6, [p4, k3] twice, p2, k1, p1, k1.

Row 30: As Row 2.

Row 31: As Row 29.

Row 32: As Row 2.

Rows 33-38: Repeat Rows 27-32.

Repeat Rows 3-38 for Center Panel, 9 times more, then rep Rows 3-25 once more.

Next Row: K1, p2, k2, [(p2tog) twice, k3] twice, [p2tog] 3 times, [k3, (p2tog) twice] twice, k2, p2, k1. (33 sts)

Purl 4 rows.

Cast off purlwise.

Panel 1: (worked over 26 sts)

Make 2 the same.

Using Dk Brown, cast on 20 sts.

Knit 4 rows.

Row 1: (*right side*) K1, p1, k1, [p2, (kf&b) 3 times, p2] twice, k1, p1, k1. (26 sts)

Row 2: K1, p2, [k2, p6, k2] twice, p2, k1.

Row 3: K1, p1, k1, p2, C6B, p4, C6F, p2, k1, p1, k1.

Row 4: As Row 2.

Rows 5, 7 and 9: K1, p1, k1, [p2, k6, p2] twice, k1, p1, k1.

Rows 6, 8 and 10: As Row 2.

Repeat Rows 3-10 for pattern, 47 times more, then rep Rows 3 and 4 once more.

Next Row: (right side) K1, p1, k1, [p2, (k2tog) 3 times, p2] twice, k1, p1, k1. (20 sts)

Knit 4 rows.

Cast off knitwise.

Panel 2: (worked over 34 sts)

Make 2 the same.

Using Grey, cast on 28 sts.

Knit 4 rows.

Next Row: (*right side*) K1, p1, k1, p4, k3, p8, k3, p4, k1, p1, k1.

Next Row: K1, p2, k4, p3, k8, p3, k4, p2, k1.

Row 1: (right side) K1, p1, k1, p4, [kf&b] 3 times, p8, [kf&b] 3 times, p4, k1, p1, k1. (34 sts)

Row 2: K1, p2, k4, p6, k8, p6, k4, p2, k1.

Row 3: K1, p1, k1, p4, C6F, p8, C6F, p4, k1, p1, k1.

Rows 4, 6 and 8: As Row 2.

Rows 5 and 7: K1, p1, k1, p4, k6, p8, k6, p4, k1, p1, k1.

Row 9: As Row 3.

Row 10: As Row 2.

Row 11: K1, p1, k1, p3, C4R, C4L, p6, C4R, C4L, p3, k1, p1, k1.

Row 12: K1, p2, k3, p3, k2, p3, k6, p3, k2, p3, k3, p2, k1.

Please Note: The Throw pictured does not show the complete width. The wide Ecru panel is the center of the Throw.

Row 13: K1, p1, k1, p2, C4R, p2, C4L, p4, C4R, p2, C4L, p2, k1, p1, k1.

Row 14: K1, p2, k2, [p3, k4] 3 times, p3, k2, p2, k1.

Row 15: K1, p1, k1, p2, k3, p4, C4L, p2, C4R, p4, k3, p2, k1, p1, k1.

Row 16: K1, p2, [k2, p3, k5, p3] twice, k2, p2, k1.

Row 17: K1, p1, k1, p2, C4L, p4, C4L, C4R, p4, C4R, p2, k1, p1, k1.

Row 18: K1, p2, k3, p3, k5, p6, k5, p3, k3, p2, k1.

Row 19: K1, p1, k1, p3, C4L, p4, C6B, p4, C4R, p3, k1, p1, k1.

Row 20: K1, p2, k4, p3, k4, p6, k4, p3, k4, p2, k1.

Row 21: K1, p1, k1, p4, [C4L, p2, C4R] twice, p4, k1, p1, k1.

Row 22: K1, p2, k5, p3, [k2, p3] 3 times, k5, p2, k1.

Row 23: K1, p1, k1, p5, C4L, C4R, p2, C4L, C4R, p5, k1, p1, k1.

Row 24: K1, p2, k6, p6, k4, p6, k6, p2, k1.

Row 25: K1, p1, k1, p6, C6F, p4, C6F, p6, k1, p1, k1.

Row 26: As Row 24.

Row 27: K1, p1, k1, p5, C4R, C4L, p2, C4R, C4L, p5, k1, p1, k1.

Row 28: K1, p2, k5, p3, [k2, p3] 3 times, k5, p2, k1.

Row 29: K1, p1, k1, p4, [C4R, p2, C4L] twice, p4, k1, p1, k1.

Row 30: K1, p2, k4, p3, k4, p6, k4, p3, k4, p2, k1.

Row 31: K1, p1, k1, p3, C4R, p4, C6B, p4, C4L, p3, k1, p1, k1.

Row 32: K1, p2, k3, p3, k5, p6, k5, p3, k3, p2, k1.

Row 33: K1, p1, k1, p2, C4R, p4, C4R, C4L, p4, C4L, p2, k1, p1, k1.

Row 34: K1, p2, k2, p3, k5, p3, k2, p3, k5, p3, k2, p2, k1.

Row 35: K1, p1, k1, p2, k3, p4, C4R, p2, C4L, p4, k3, p2, k1, p1, k1.

Row 36: K1, p2, k2, p3, [k4, p3] 3 times, k2, p2, k1.

Row 37: K1, p1, k1, p2, C4L, p2, C4R, p4, C4L, p2, C4R, p2, k1, p1, k1.

Row 38: K1, p2, k3, p3, k2, p3, k6, p3, k2, p3, k3, p2, k1.

Row 39: K1, p1, k1, p3, C4L, C4R, p6, C4L, C4R, p3, k1, p1, k1.

Row 40: K1, p2, k4, p6, k8, p6, k4, p2, k1.

Repeat Rows 3-40 for pattern 9 times more, then Rows 3-10 once more.

Next Row: K1, p1, k1, p4, [k2tog] 3 times, p8, [k2tog] 3 times, p4, k1, p1, k1. (28) sts

Next Row: K1, p2, k4, p3, k8, p3, k4, p2, k1.

Next Row: K1, p1, k1, p4, k3, p8, k3, p4, k1, p1, k1.

Knit 4 rows.

Cast off knitwise.

Panel 3: (worked over 26 sts)

Make 2 the same.

Using Dk Brown, cast on 22 sts.

Knit 4 rows.

Row 1: (*right side*) K1, p1, k1, p3, [kf&b] twice, p2, k2, p2, [kf&b] twice, p3, k1, p1, k1. (26 sts)

Row 2: K1, p2, k3, p4, k2, p2, k2, p4, k3, p2, k1.

Rows 3, 5, 7 and 9: K1, p1, k1, p3, k4, p2, k2, p2, k4, p3, k1, p1, k1.

Rows 4, 6, 8 and 10: As Row 2.

Row 11: K1, p1, k1, p3, C4F, p2, k2, p2, C4B, p3, k1, p1, k1.

Row 12: As Row 2.

Row 13: K1, p1, k1, p3, k2, C4F, k2, C4B, k2, p3, k1, p1, k1.

Row 14: K1, p2, k3, p 14, k3, p2, k1.

Row 15: K1, p1, k1, p3, k4, C3L, C3R, k4, p3, k1, p1, k1.

Row 16: K1, p2, k3, p4, k2, T2FP, k2, p4, k3, p2, k1.

Row 17: As Row 3.

Row 18: As Row 2.

Repeat Rows 3-18 for pattern, 23 times more, then Rows 3-6 once more.

Next Row: K1, p1, k1, p3, [k2tog] twice, p2, k2, p2, [k2tog] twice, p3, k1, p1, k1. (22 sts)

Knit 4 rows.

Cast off knitwise.

Panel 4: (worked over 20 sts)

Make 2 the same.

Using Ecru, cast on 17 sts.

Knit 4 rows.

Row 1: (*right side*) K1, p1, k1, p4, [kf&b] 3 times, p4, k1, p1, k1. (20 sts)

Row 2: K1, p2, k4, p6, k4, p2, k1.

Row 3: K1, p1, k1, p4, C6B, p4, k1, p1, k1.

Row 4: As Row 2.

Row 5: K1, p1, k1, p4, k6, p4, k1, p1, k1.

Row 6: As Row 2.

Row 7: As Row 3.

Row 8: As Row 2.

Row 9: K1, p1, k1, p3, T3B, k2, T3F, p3, k1, p1, k1.

Row 10: K1, p2, k3, [p2, k1] twice, p2, k3, p2, k1.

Row 11: K1, p1, k1, p2, T3B, p1, k2, p1, T3F, p2, k1, p1, k1.

Row 12: K1, p2, [k2, p2] 4 times, k1.

Rows 13, 15 and 17: K1, p1, k1, [p2, k2] 3 times, p2, k1, p1, k1.

Rows 14, 16 and 18: As Row 12.

Row 19: K1, p1, k1, p2, T3F, p1, k2, p1, T3B, p2, k1, p1, k1.

Row 20: As Row 10.

Row 21: K1, p1, k1, p3, T3F, k2, T3B, p3, k1, p1, k1.

Row 22: As Row 2.

Repeat Rows 3-22 for pattern 18 times more, then rep Rows 3-8 once more.

Next Row: K1, p1, k1, p4, [k2tog] 3 times, p4, ,k1, p1, k1. (17 sts)

Knit 4 rows.

Cast off knitwise.

Panel 5: (worked over 34 sts)

Make 2 the same.

Using Lt Brown, cast on 28 sts.

Knit 4 rows.

Row 1: K1, p1, k1, [p4, (kf&b) twice] 3 times, p4, k1, p1, k1. (34 sts)

Row 2: K1, p2, k4, [p4, k4] 3 times, p2, k1.

Row 3: (*right side*) K1, p1, k1, p4, k4, p4, C4B, p4, k4, p4, k1, p1, k1.

Row 4: As Row 2.

Row 5: K1, p1, k1, p4, [k4, p4] 3 times, k1, p1, k1.

Row 6: As Row 2.

Row 7: K1, p1, k1, p4, T4F, p4, C4B, p4, T4B, p4, k1, p1, k1.

Row 8: K1, p2, k6, p2, k4, p4, k4, p2, k6, p2, k1.

Row 9: K1, p1, k1, p6, [T4F, T4B] twice, p6, k1, p1, k1.

Row 10: K1, p2, k8, p4, k4, p4, k8, p2, k1.

Row 11: K1, p1, k1, p8, C4B, p4, C4F, p8, k1, p1, k1.

Row 12: As Row 10.

Row 13: K1, p1, k1, p6, C4B, T4F, T4B, C4F, p6, k1, p1, k1.

Row 14: K1, p2, k6, p4, [k2, p4] twice, k6, p2, k1.

Row 15: K1, p1, k1, p4, T4B, k2, p2, C4B, p2, k2, T4F, p4, k1, p1, k1.

Row 16: K1, p2, k4, [p2, k2] twice, p4, [k2, p2] twice, k4, p2, k1.

Row 17: K1, p1, k1, p4, [k2, p2] twice, k4, [p2, k2] twice, p4, k1, p1, k1.

Row 18: As Row 16.

Row 19: K1, p1, k1, p4, k2, T4B, p2, C4B, p2, T4F, k2, p4, k1, p1, k1.

Row 20: As Row 2.

Row 21: K1, p1, k1, p4, T4B, p2, T4B, T4F, p2, T4F, p4, k1, p1, k1.

Row 22: K1, p2, [k4, p2] 5 times, k1.

Row 23: K1, p1, k1, p2, T4B, p2, C4B, p4, C4F, p2, T4F, p2, k1, p1, k1.

Row 24: K1, p2, k2, p2, k4, [p4, k4] twice, p2, k2, p2, k1.

Row 25: K1, p1, k1, p2, k2, p2, T4B, k2, p4, k2, T4F, p2, k2, p2, k1, p1, k1.

Row 26: K1, p2, [k2, p2] 3 times, k4, [p2, k2] 3 times, p2, k1.

Row 27: K1, p1, k1, [p2, k2] 3 times, p4, [k2, p2] 3 times, k1, p1, k1.

Row 28: As Row 26.

Row 29: K1, p1, k1, [p2, k2] twice, T4B, p4, T4F, [k2, p2] twice, k1, p1, k1.

Row 30: K1, [p2, k2] twice, p4, k8, p4, [k2, p2] twice, k1.

Row 31: K1, p1, k1, p2, T4F, T4B, p8, T4F, T4B, p2, k1, p1, k1.

Row 32: K1, p2, k4, p4, k 12, p4, k4, p2, k1.

Row 33: K1, p1, k1, p4, C4F, p 12, C4B, p4, k1, p1, k1.

Row 34: As Row 32.

Row 35: K1, p1, k1, p4, k4, p 12, k4, p4, k1, p1, k1.

Row 36: As Row 32.

Row 37: As Row 33.

Row 38: As Row 32.

Row 39: K1, p1, k1, p2, T4B, C4F, p8, C4B, T4F, p2, k1, p1, k1.

Row 40: As Row 30.

Row 41: K1, p1, k1, [p2, k2] twice, T4F, p4, T4B, [k2, p2] twice, k1, p1, k1.

Row 42: As Row 26.

Row 43: As Row 27.

Row 44: As Row 26.

Row 45: K1, p1, k1, p2, k2, p2, T4F, k2, p4, k2, T4B, p2, k2, p2, k1, p1, k1.

Row 46: As Row 24.

Row 47: K1, p1, k1, p2, T4F, p2, T4F, p4, T4B, p2, T4B, p2, k1, p1, k1.

Row 48: As Row 22.

Row 49: K1, p1, k1, p4, C4F, p2, T4F, T4B, p2, C4B, p4, k1, p1, k1.

Row 50: As Row 2.

Row 51: K1, p1, k1, p4, k2, T4F, p2, C4B, p2, T4B, k2, p4, k1, p1, k1.

Row 52: As Row 16.

Row 53: As Row 17.

Row 54: As Row 16.

Row 55: K1, p1, k1, p4, T4F, k2, p2, C4B, p2, k2, T4B, p4, k1, p1, k1.

Row 56: As Row 14.

Row 57: K1, p1, k1, p6, [T4F, T4B] twice, p6, k1, p1, k1.

Row 58: As Row 10.

Row 59: K1, p1, k1, p8, C4F, p4, C4B, p8, k1, p1, k1.

Row 60: As Row 10.

Row 61: K1, p1, k1, p6, [T4B, T4F] twice, p6, k1, p1, k1.

Row 62: K1, p2, k6, p2, k4, p4, k4, p2, k6, p2, k1.

Row 63: K1, p1, k1, p4, [C4B, p4] twice, C4F, p4, k1, p1, k1.

Row 64: As Row 2.

Row 65: As Row 5.

Row 66: As Row 2.

Repeat Rows 3-66 for pattern 5 times more.

Next Row: Work in pattern to end, dec 6 sts evenly across. (28 sts)

Knit 4 rows.

Cast off knitwise.

Sew panels together in order as illustrated.

Placement Illustration

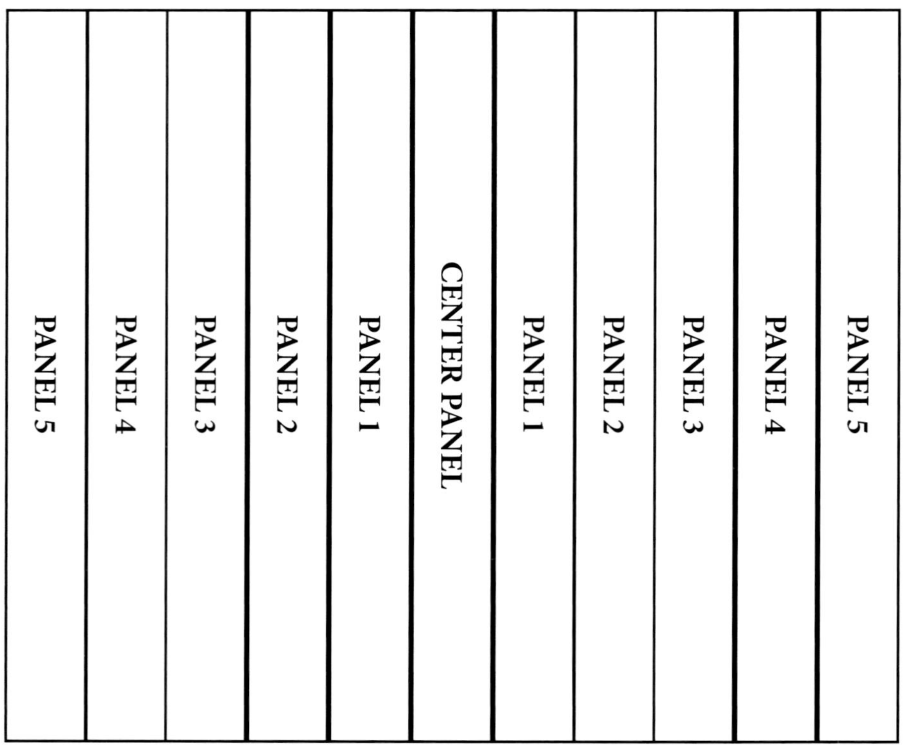

Dreams of Ireland

Shown on page 13.

INTERMEDIATE

SHOPPING LIST

Yarn (Worsted Weight) MEDIUM 4

Aran Irish Twist ***or*** Tweed

[4 ounces, 205 yards]

(113 grams, 187 meters) per skein]:

☐ 12 skeins

Knitting Needles

☐ Size 9 (5.50 mm)

or size needed for gauge

Crochet Hook

☐ Size H-8 (5.00 mm)

for fringe only

SIZE INFORMATION

Finished: 42.5" x 60" [108 x 152.5 cm]

GAUGE INFORMATION

Honeycomb (between cables) = 8.5" [21.5 cm] wide,

Diamonds & Bobbles (between cables) = 5.5" [14 cm] wide

Puff st (between cables) = 2.5" [6.5 cm] wide

Braided Cable (between outer cables) = 2.5" [6.5 cm] wide

Smocked Section (between cables) = 5.5" [14 cm] wide

Seed st borders = 1.5" [4 cm] wide,

and 20 rows = 4" [10 cm]

all using **suggested** needles or any size needles which will give the correct gauge.

STITCH GUIDE

sl 3P Slip 3 sts purlwise to right-hand needle

C3F Slip next 2 sts onto cable needle and hold to front of work, k1 from left-hand needle, then k2 from cable needle.

T5F Slip next 2 sts onto cable needle and hold to front of work, k2, p1 from left-hand needle, then k2 from cable needle.

T3B Slip next st onto cable needle and hold to back of work, k2 from left-hand needle, then p1 from cable needle.

T3F Slip next 2 sts onto cable needle and hold to front of work, p1 from left-hand needle, then k2 from cable needle.

C4F Slip next 2 sts onto a cable needle and hold to front of work, k2 from left-hand needle, then k2 from cable needle.

C4B Slip next 2 sts onto a cable needle and hold to back of work, k2 from left-hand needle, then k2 from cable needle.

Bobble (K1, [yo, k1] twice) all in next st, turn, p5, turn, k5, turn, p1, p3tog, p1, turn, sl 1, k2tog, psso.

C3R Slip next 2 sts onto cable needle and hold to back of work, k1 from left-hand needle, then k2 from cable needle.

C3L Slip next st onto cable needle and hold to front of work, k2 from left-hand needle, then k1 from cable needle.

SP Insert right-hand needle in 3rd st and draw through a loop, then knit the first and 2nd sts, drop 3rd st off needle.

DYO Drop yarn over, creating a long st.

C6F Slip next 3 sts onto cable needle and hold to front of work, k3 from left-hand needle, then k3 from cable needle.

C6B Slip next 3 sts onto cable needle and hold to back of work, k3 from left-hand needle, then k3 from cable needle.

INSTRUCTIONS

Center Panel:

Cast on 78 sts. Knit 5 rows.

Base Row: (*inc row, wrong side*) K2, p3, PM, k8, inc one st in next st purlwise, k1, inc one st in next st purlwise, k8, PM,

p3, k2, [inc one st in next st purlwise] 20 times, k2, p3, PM,

k8, inc one st in next st purlwise, k1, inc one st in next st purlwise, k8, PM, p3, k2. (102 sts)

Now work patterns as follows, slipping all M's on each row:

Row 1: (*right side*) P2, C3F, p8, T5F, p8, C3F, p2, k 40, p2, C3F, p8, T5F, p8, C3F, p2.
Row 2: K2, sl 3P, k8, p2, k1, p2, k8, sl 3P, k2, p 40, k2, sl 3P, k8, p2, k1, p2, k8, sl 3P, k2.
Row 3: P2, C3F, p7, T3B, p1, T3F, p7, C3F, p2, [C4B, C4F] 5 times, p2, C3F, p7, T3B, p1, T3F, p7, C3F, p2.
Row 4: K2, sl 3P, k7, p2, k3, p2, k7, sl 3P, k2, p 40, k2, sl 3P, k7, p2, k3, p2, k7, sl 3P, k2.
Row 5: P2, C3F, p6, T3B, p3, T3F, p6, C3F, p2, k 40, p2, C3F, p6, T3B, p3, T3F, p6, C3F, p2.
Row 6: K2, sl 3P, k6, p2, k5, p2, k6, sl 3P, k2, p 40, k2, sl 3P, k6, p2, k5, p2, k6, sl 3P, k2.
Row 7: P2, C3F, p5, T3B, p2, Bobble, p2, T3F, p5, C3F, p2, [C4F, C4B] 5 times, p2, C3F, p5, T3B, p2, Bobble, p2, T3F, p5, C3F, p2.
Row 8: K2, sl 3P, k5, p2, k7, p2, k5, sl 3P, k2, p 40, k2, sl 3P, k5, p2, k7, p2, k5, sl 3P, k2.
Row 9: P2, C3F, p4, T3B, p7, T3F, p4, C3F, p2, k 40, p2, C3F, p4, T3B, p7, T3F, p4, C3F, p2.
Row 10: K2, sl 3P, k4, p2, k9, p2, k4, sl 3P, k2, p 40, k2, sl 3P, k4, p2, k9, p2, k4, sl 3P, k2.
Row 11: P2, C3F, p3, T3B, p2, Bobble, p3, Bobble, p2, T3F, p3, C3F, p2, [C4B, C4F] 5 times, p2, C3F, p3, T3B, p2, Bobble, p3, Bobble, p2, T3F, p3, C3F, p2.
Row 12: K2, sl 3P, k3, p2, k 11, p2, k3, sl 3P, k2, p 40, k2, sl 3P, k3, p2, k 11, p2, k3, sl 3P, k2.
Row 13: P2, C3F, p3, k2, p 11, k2, p3, C3F, p2, k 40, p2, C3F, p3, k2, p 11, k2, p3, C3F, p2.
Row 14: K2, sl 3P, k3, p2, k 11, p2, k3, sl 3P, k2, p 40, k2, sl 3P, k3, p2, k 11, p2, k3, sl 3P, k2.
Row 15: P2, C3F, p3, T3F, p2, Bobble, p3, Bobble, p2, T3B, p3, C3F, p2, [C4F, C4B] 5 times, p2, C3F, p3, T3F, p2, Bobble, p3, Bobble, p2, T3B, p3, C3F, p2.
Row 16: K2, sl 3P, k4, p2, k9, p2, k4, sl 3P, k2, p 40, k2, sl 3P, k4, p2, k9, p2, k4, sl 3P, k2.
Row 17: P2, C3F, p4, T3F, p7, T3B, p4, C3F, p2, k 40, p2, C3F, p4, T3F, p7, T3B, p4, C3F, p2.
Row 18: K2, sl 3P, k5, p2, k7, p2, k5, sl 3P, k2, p 40, k2, sl 3P, k5, p2, k7, p2, k5, sl 3P, k2.
Row 19: P2, C3F, p5, T3F, p2, Bobble, p2, T3B, p5, C3F, p2, [C4B, C4F] 5 times, p2, C3F, p5, T3F, p2, Bobble, p2, T3B, p5, C3F, p2.
Row 20: K2, sl 3P, k6, p2, k5, p2, k6, sl 3P, k2, p 40, k2, sl 3P, k6, p2, k5, p2, k6, sl 3P, k2.
Row 21: P2, C3F, p6, T3F, p3, T3B, p6, C3F, p2, k 40, p2, C3F, p6, T3F, p3, T3B, p6, C3F, p2.
Row 22: K2, sl 3P, k7, p2, k3, p2, k7, sl 3P, k2, p 40, k2, sl 3P, k7, p2, k3, p2, k7, sl 3P, k2.
Row 23: P2, C3F, p7, T3F, p1, T3B, p7, C3F, p2, [C4F, C4B] 5 times, p2, C3F, p7, T3F, p1, T3B, p7, C3F, p2.
Row 24: K2, sl 3P, k8, p2, k1, p2, k8, sl 3P, k2, p 40, k2, sl 3P, k8, p2, k1, p2, k8, sl 3P, k2.
Repeat Rows 1-24 eleven times more (288 rows of pattern).
Note: On next row, remove all M's as you come to them.
Next Row: K13, k2tog, k1, k2tog, k13, (k2tog) 20 times, k13, k2tog, k1, k2tog, k13. (78 sts)
Knit 5 rows. Cast off all sts.

Right Side Panel:
Cast on 55 sts. Knit 5 rows.
Base Row: (*inc row, wrong side*) [K2, p3] twice, PM, k2, [p1, inc one st in next st purlwise] 3 times, k2, PM, p3, PM, k2, p 20, k2, PM, p3, k1, [p1, k1] twice. (58 sts)
Now work in pattern as follows, slipping M's on every row:
Row 1: K1, [p1, k1] twice, C3F, p2, k1, [yo, k5, yo, k1] twice, yo, k5, yo, k2, p2, C3F, p2, k9, p2, C3F, p2, SP, p2.
Row 2: K2, p1, (k1, p1, k1) in next st, p1, k2, sl 3P, k2, p9, k2, sl 3P, k2, p1, sl 1, DYO, p4, [sl 1, DYO] twice, p4, [sl 1, DYO] twice, p4, sl 1, DYO, p1, k2, sl 3P, k1, [p1, k1] twice.
Row 3: K1, [p1, k1] twice, C3F, p2, k1, [C3L, C3R] 3 times, k1, p2, C3F, p2, C6F, k3, p2, C3F, p2, k1, p3, k1, p2.

Designed By: Emily Armstrong

Row 4: K2, p1, p3tog, p1, k2,
sl 3P, k2, p9, k2, sl 3P,
k2, p 20, k2, sl 3P, k1, [p1, k1] twice.

Row 5: K1, [p1, k1] twice, C3F, p2,
k3, [yo, k1, yo, k5] twice, yo, k1, yo, k4,
p2, C3F, p2, k9, p2, C3F, p2, SP, p2.

Row 6: K2, p1, (k1, p1, k1) in next st,
p1, k2, sl 3P, k2, p9, k2, sl 3P,
k2, p3, [sl 1, DYO] twice, p4, [sl 1, DYO]
twice, p4, [sl 1, DYO] twice, p3, k2,
sl 3P, k1, [p1, k1] twice.

Row 7: K1, [p1, k1] twice, C3F, p2,
k1, [C3R, C3L] 3 times, k1, p2, C3F, p2,
k3, C6B, p2, C3F, p2, k1, p3, k1, p2.

Row 8: K2, p1, p3tog, p1, k2,
sl 3P, k2, p9, k2, sl 3P, k2, p 20, k2,
sl 3P, k1, [p1, k1] twice.

Repeat these 8 rows of pattern 35
times more (288 rows).

Next Row: *(remove M's as they come)*
K 37, [k1, k2tog] 3 times, k to end.
Knit 5 rows. Cast off all sts.

Left Side Panel:

Cast on 55 sts. Knit 5 rows.

Base Row: (*inc row, wrong side*)
K1, [p1, k1] twice, p3, PM,
k2, p 20, k2, PM,
p3, k2, [p1, inc one st in next st
purlwise] 3 times, k2, PM,
[p3, k2] twice. (58 sts)

Now work patterns as follows,
slipping M's on every row:

Row 1: (right side) P2, SP, p2, C3F,
p2, k9, p2, C3F,
p2, k1, [yo, k5, yo, k1] twice, yo, k5, yo,
k2, p2, C3F, k1, [p1, k1] twice.

Row 2: K1, [p1, k1] twice, sl 3P,
k2, p1, sl 1, DYO, p4, [sl 1, DYO] twice,
p4, [sl 1, DYO] twice, p4, sl 1, DYO,
p1, k2, sl 3P, k2, p9, k2, sl 3P,
k2, p1, (k1, p1, k1) in next st, p1, k2.

Row 3: P2, k1, p3, k1, p2, C3F,
p2, C6F, k3, p2, C3F,
p2, k1, [C3L, C3R] 3 times, k1, p2,
C3F, k1, [p1, k1] twice.

Row 4: K1, [p1, k1] twice, sl 3P,
k2, p 20, k2, sl 3P,
k2, p9, k2, sl 3P, k2, p1, p3tog, p1, k2.

Row 5: P2, SP, p2, C3F,
p2, k9, p2, C3F,
p2, k3, [yo, k1, yo, k5] twice, yo, k1, yo,
k4, p2, C3F, k1, [p1, k1] twice.

Row 6: K1, [p1, k1] twice, sl 3P,
k2, p3, [sl 1, DYO] twice, p4, [sl 1, DYO]
twice, p4, [sl 1, DYO] twice, p3, k2,
sl 3P, k2, p9, k2, sl 3P,
k2, p1, (k1, p1, k1) in next st, p1, k2.

Row 7: P2, k1, p3, k1, p2, C3F,
p2, k3, C6B, p2, C3F,
p2, k1, [C3R, C3L] 3 times, k1, p2,
C3F, k1, [p1, k1] twice.

Row 8: K1, [p1, k1] twice, sl 3P,
k2, p 20, k2, sl 3P,
k2, p9, k2, sl 3P, k2, p1, p3tog, p1, k2.

Repeat these 8 rows of pattern 35
times more (288 rows).

Note: On next row, remove all M's as
you come to them.

Next Row: K 12, [k1, k2tog] 3 times,
k to end.
Knit 5 rows. Cast off all sts.

To Complete:

Sew 3 panels together lengthwise.

Fringe: Cut strands of yarn 12"
[30.5 cm] long. Hold 4 strands of yarn
and fold in half. Use crochet hook
to pull through knit rows at end of
afghan, and pass ends through to
form knot. Repeat across row. Repeat
for other end of afghan.

Set up of Patterns

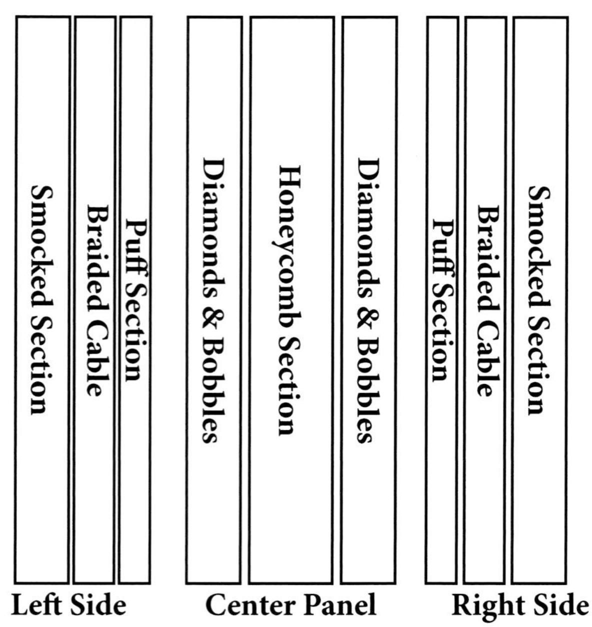

Lilies & Lace Throw

Shown on page 17.

INTERMEDIATE

SHOPPING LIST

Yarn (Dk/Sport Weight) LIGHT 3

Mary Maxim Ultra Mellowspun
[1.75 ounces, 174 yards
(50 grams, 160 meters) per ball]:

- ☐ Robin's Egg 15 balls

Knitting Needle

36" (90 cm) Circular Needle

- ☐ Size 6 (4.0 mm) or size needed for gauge

SIZE INFORMATION

Finished: 43" x 57" [109 x 145 cm]

GAUGE INFORMATION

Leaf Patterns A and B:
One repeat (10 sts) = 2" [5 cm] and
32 rows (4 rep) = 4" [10 cm] and
Lily Pattern:
One repeat (23 sts) = 4.25" [11 cm]
and 28 rows = 5" [12.5 cm]
both using **suggested** needle or any size needle needed to obtain correct gauge.

STITCH GUIDE

M1 Using tip of left-hand needle, pick up horizontal strand between st just worked and next st, then using right-hand needle, k1 through back of loop.

ssk Slip next 2 sts knitwise, one at a time, to right-hand needle, then insert left-hand needle through fronts of both sts, from back to front, and k2tog as usual.

MB (K1, k1 tbl, k1) all in next st, turn work and k3, turn & sl 1, k2tog, psso.

CL3 or CL5 With yarn in back, slip 3 (or 5) sts onto cable needle, wrap yarn clockwise 2 times around these sts, then with yarn in back, slip the same stitches onto right-hand needle.

p2sso: Pass both slipped sts over last st on right hand needle.

Note: When working patterns across the body of the Throw, please note that the placement of patterns is not the same working from each edge.

Leaf Pattern A: (worked over 10 sts)
Row 1: (*wrong side*) P 10.
Row 2: K6, sl 1, ssk, psso, yo, k1, yo.
Rows 3, 5 and 7: As Row 1.
Row 4: K4, sl 1, ssk, psso, k1, yo, k1, yo, k1.
Row 6: K2, sl 1, ssk, psso, k2, yo, k1, yo, k2.
Row 8: Sl 1, ssk, psso, k3, yo, k1, yo, k3.
Repeat these 8 rows for pattern.

Leaf Pattern B: (worked over 10 sts)
Row 1: (*wrong side*) P 10.
Row 2: Yo, k1, yo, sl 1, k2tog, psso, k6.
Rows 3, 5 and 7: As Row 1.
Row 4: K1, yo, k1, yo, k1, sl 1, k2tog, psso, k4.
Row 6: K2, yo, k1, yo, k2, sl 1, k2tog, psso, k2.
Row 8: K3, yo, k1, yo, k3, sl 1, k2tog, psso.
Repeat these 8 rows for pattern.

Lily Pattern: (worked over 23 sts)
Row 1 and every alternate row: (*wrong side*) P 23.
Row 2: Ssk, k6, [yo, k1] twice, sl 1, k2tog, psso, [k1, yo] twice, k6, k2tog.
Row 4: Ssk, k5, yo, k1, yo, k2, sl 1, k2tog, psso, k2, yo, k1, yo, k5, k2tog.
Row 6: Ssk, k4, yo, k1, yo, MB, k2, sl 1, k2tog, psso, k2, MB, yo, k1, yo, k4, k2tog.
Row 8: Ssk, k3, yo, k1, yo, MB, k3, sl 1, k2tog, psso, k3, MB, yo, k1, yo, k3, k2tog.
Row 10: Ssk, k2, yo, k1, yo, MB, k4, sl 1, k2tog, psso, k4, MB, yo, k1, yo, k2, k2tog.
Row 12: Ssk, [k1, yo] twice, MB, k5, sl 1, k2tog, psso, k5, MB, [yo, k1] twice, k2tog.
Row 14: Ssk, yo, k1, yo, MB, k6, sl 1, k2tog, psso, k6, MB, yo, k1, yo, k2tog.
Rep Rows 1-14 for pattern.

Lace Pattern: (worked over 5 sts)
Row 1: (*wrong side*): Purl.
Row 2: K2tog, yo, k1, yo, sl 1, k1, psso.
Repeat these 2 rows for pattern.

INSTRUCTIONS

**Cast on 265 sts and work Border pattern as follows:

Row 1: (*right side*) K1, *yo, [k1, p3] 5 times, k1, yo, k1; rep from * to end. (289 sts)

Row 2: P3, *[k3, p1] 4 times, k3, p5; rep from * across ending last rep with p3. (289 sts)

Row 3: K1, *yo, k1, yo, [k1, p3] 5 times, [k1, yo] twice, k1; rep from * across. (337 sts)

Row 4: P5, *[k3, p1] 4 times, k3, p9; rep from * across, ending last rep with p5.

Row 5: K1, *yo, k1, yo, ssk, yo, [k1, p2tog, p1] 5 times, k1, yo, k2tog, [yo, k1] twice; rep from * to end. (325 sts)

Row 6: P7, *[k2, p1] 4 times, k2, p13; rep from * across, ending last rep with p7.

Row 7: K1, *k1, [yo, ssk] twice, yo, [k1, p2] 5 times, k1, yo, [k2tog, yo] twice, k2; rep from * to end. (349 sts)

Row 8: P8, *[k2, p1] 4 times, k2, p15; rep from * across, ending last rep with p8.

Row 9: K2, *[yo, k2tog] twice, yo, k1, yo, [k1, p2tog] 5 times, [k1, yo] twice, [ssk, yo] twice, k3; rep from * across, ending last rep with k2. (337 sts)

Rows 10 and 12: P 10, *[k1, p1] 4 times, k1, p 19; rep from * across, ending last rep with p10. (337 sts)

Row 11: Ssk, *[yo, k2tog] 3 times, k1, yo, [k1, p1] 5 times, k1, yo, k1, [ssk, yo] 3 times, sl 2, k1, p2sso; rep from * across, ending last rep with k2tog *instead of* sl 2, k1, p2sso.

Row 13: K1, *[k2tog, yo] twice, k2tog, k2, yo, (ssk) twice, sl 1, k2tog, psso, (k2tog) twice, yo, k2, ssk, [yo, ssk] twice, k1; rep from * across. (265 sts)

Row 14: P9, CL5, *p7, CL3, p7, CL5; rep from * to last 9 sts, p9. (265 sts)**

Reverse St st Ridge:

Row 1: Purl, inc one st at center of row. (266 sts)

Rows 2, 4 and 6: Knit.

Rows 3 and 5: Purl.

Row 7: Knit.

Now set patterns in place for body of Blanket as follows:

Row 1: (*wrong side*) Sl 1, p1, [k1, p1] 3 times, PM,
*work Row 1 of Leaf Pattern A over next 10 sts, PM
work Row 1 of Lace Pattern over next 5 sts, PM
work Row 1 of Leaf Pattern B over next 10 sts, PM
work Row 1 of Lily Pattern over next 23 sts, PM; rep from * to last 18 sts, work Row 1 of Leaf Pattern A over next 10 sts, place PM, [p1, k1] 4 times.

Row 2: (*right side*) Sl 1, k1, [p1, k1] 3 times, sl M,
work Row 2 of Leaf Pattern A over next 10 sts, sl M,
*work Row 2 of Lily Pattern over next 23 sts, sl M,
work Row 2 of Leaf Pattern B over next 10 sts, sl M,
work Row 2 of Lace Pattern over next 5 sts, sl M,
work Row 2 of Leaf Pattern A over next 10 sts, sl M; rep from * to last 8 sts, sl M, [k1, p1] 4 times.

Row 3: Sl 1, p1, [k1, p1] 3 times, sl M,
*work Row 3 of Leaf Pattern A to next M, sl M,
work Row 1 of Lace Pattern to next M, sl M,
work Row 3 of Leaf Pattern B to next M, sl M,
work Row 3 of Lily Pattern to next M, sl M; rep from * to last 18 sts, work Row 3 of Leaf Pattern A to next M, sl M, [p1, k1] 4 times.

Now continue to work correct rows of patterns, keeping first 8 sts and last 8 sts in ribbing as set, until piece measures 55" [139.5 cm] from cast on edge, ending after a right side row.

Next Row: (*wrong side*) Work first 8 sts in ribbing as set, p to last 8 sts dec one st at center of row, work last 8 sts in ribbing. (265 sts)

Next Row: Purl.

Next Row: Knit.

Repeat these last 2 rows once more.

Next Row: Knit.

Optional: At this point a second Border will be made. You can either cast off knitwise and then sew the second Border to the cast off edge; or, slip these sts onto a spare needle in order to graft the second Border to the blanket.

Second Border:

Work as given from ** to **.
Cast off loosely knitwise.
Holding both pieces with cast off ends side by side, wrong sides tog, sew Second Border to blanket.

If Grafting, lay both pieces on a flat surface with right sides facing up. Using a long piece of yarn, graft Second Border to body of Blanket.

How to Graft

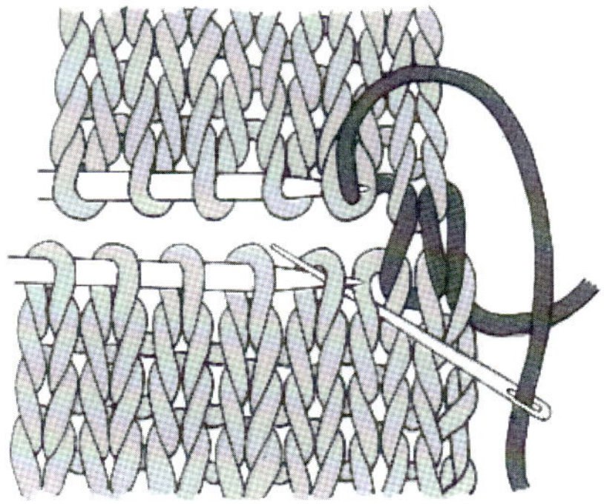

Crimson Comfort

INTERMEDIATE

SHOPPING LIST

Yarn (Worsted Weight) MEDIUM 4

Mary Maxim Best Value
[6 ounces, 342 yards
(170 grams, 313 meters) per skein]:

☐ Rich Red 6 skeins

Knitting Needle:

36" (90 cm) Circular Needle

☐ Size 8 (5.00 mm)

or size needed for gauge

SIZE INFORMATION

Finished: 52.5" x 60" [133 x 152.5 cm]

GAUGE INFORMATION

32 sts (2 pattern repeats) to 7" [17.5 cm] and 36 rows to 6" [15 cm], measured over pattern, using **suggested** needle or any size needle which will give the correct gauge.

STITCH GUIDE

ssk Slip next 2 sts knitwise, one at a time, to right-hand needle, insert left-hand needle through fronts of both sts from back to front and k2tog as usual.

Cr6B Slip next 4 sts onto cable needle and hold to back of work, k2 from left-hand needle, then slip 2 purled sts to left-hand needle and p2, k2 from cable needle.

Cr6F Slip next 4 sts onto cable needle and hold to front of work, k2 from left-hand needle, then slip 2 purled sts to left-hand needle and p2, k2 from cable needle.

INSTRUCTIONS

Cast on 224 sts and knit 16 rows.

Next Row: (*wrong side*) K8, place a marker, p to last 8 sts, inc 16 sts evenly across, place a marker, k8. (240 sts).

Now keeping the first 8 sts and last 8 sts outside markers in Garter st - every row k (sl markers every row), work pattern over center 224 sts as follows:

Row 1: (*right side*) *P1, k1, yo, ssk, p8, k2tog, yo, k1, p1; rep from * to end.

Row 2 and every other row following: Work sts as they appear, k the knit sts and p the purl sts and yo's.

Row 3: *P1, k2, yo, ssk, p6, k2tog, yo, k2, p1; rep from * to end.

Row 5: *P1, k3, yo, ssk, p4, k2tog, yo, k3, p1; rep from * to end.

Row 7: *P1, k4, yo, ssk, p2, k2tog, yo, k4, p1; rep from * to end.

Row 9: *P1, yo, ssk, k4, p2, k4, k2tog, yo, p1; rep from * to end.

Row 11: *P2, yo, ssk, k3, p2, k3, k2tog, yo, p2; rep from * to end.

Row 13: *P3, yo, ssk, k2, p2, k2, k2tog, yo, p3; rep from * to end.

Row 15: *P4, yo, ssk, k1, p2, k1, k2tog, yo, p4; rep from * to end.

Row 17: *P5, Cr6F, p5; rep from * to end.

Row 19: *P4, k2tog, yo, k1, p2, k1, yo, ssk, p4; rep from * to end.

Row 21: *P3, k2tog, yo, k2, p2, k2, yo, ssk, p3; rep from * to end.

Row 23: *P2, k2tog, yo, k3, p2, k3, yo, ssk, p2; rep from * to end.

Row 25: *P1, k2tog, yo, k4, p2, k4, yo, ssk, p1; rep from * to end.

Row 27: *P1, k4, k2tog, yo, p2, yo, ssk, k4, p1; rep from * to end.

Row 29: *P1, k3, k2tog, yo, p4, yo, ssk, k3, p1; rep from * to end.

Row 31: *P1, k2, k2tog, yo, p6, yo, ssk, k2, p1; rep from * to end.

Row 33: *P1, k1, k2tog, yo, p8, yo, ssk, k1, p1; rep from * to end.

Row 35: P1, k2, p5, *p5, Cr6B, p5; rep from * to last 8 sts, p5, k2, p1.

Row 36: Repeat Row 2.

Repeat these 36 rows for pattern 8 times more (piece should measure 55.75" [141.5 cm] from beg), and dec 16 sts evenly between markers on last row worked. (224 sts)

Knit 16 rows.

Cast off loosely knitwise.

Designed By: Billie Birchfield

Paneled Lace Throw

INTERMEDIATE

SHOPPING LIST

Yarn (Light Worsted)

LIGHT 3

Mary Maxim Milan

[3.5 ounces, 219 yards

(100 grams, 200 meters) per ball]:

☐ Opulia 9 balls

Knitting Needles

☐ Size 9 (5.50 mm)

or size needed for gauge

SIZE INFORMATION

Finished: 40" x 48" [101.5 x 122 cm]

GAUGE INFORMATION

One pattern repeat (18 sts) to 3.25" [8 cm] and 16 rows to 2.5" [6.5 cm], measured over pattern using **suggested** needles or any size needles which will give the correct gauge.

STITCH GUIDE

See Page 29.

INSTRUCTIONS

Panel: (make 5)

Cast on 44 sts and knit 2 rows.

Now work Lace pattern as follows:

Row 1: (*right side*) Knit.

Row 2: K5, p to last 5 sts, k5.

Row 3: K4, *[k2tog] 3 times, [yo, k1] 6 times, [k2tog] 3 times; rep from * to last 4 sts, k4.

Row 4: Knit.

Repeat these 4 rows for pattern 76 times more.

Knit one row.

Cast off knitwise.

Blocking:

Lay each panel out on a flat surface as they are completed and pin to correct dimensions.

Cover with a fairly damp towel or sheet. Apply some pressure to transfer moisture through to the panel.

Leave until towel or sheet are dry.

Remove and allow the panel to dry.

To Assemble:

Lay panels out side by side, as desired, and sew together neatly.

Vertical Zigzag Throw

INTERMEDIATE

SHOPPING LIST

Yarn (Worsted Weight) MEDIUM 4

Mary Maxim Starlette

[3.5 ounces, 180 yards

(100 grams, 165 meters) per ball]:

- ☐ Teal 14 balls

Knitting Needle

36" (90 cm) Circular Needle

- ☐ Size 9 (5.50 mm)

  or size needed for gauge

SIZE INFORMATION

Finished: 48" x 60" [122 x 152.5 cm]

GAUGE INFORMATION

One repeat (21 sts) to 4.5" [11.5 cm] and 13 rows to 1.75" [4.5 cm] measured over pattern without any stretching, using **suggested** needle, or any size needle which will give the correct stitch gauge.

STITCH GUIDE

SK2P Slip next st knitwise, k2tog from left needle, then pass slipped st over rem st of k2tog.

ssk Slip next 2 sts knitwise, one at a time to right needle, then insert left needle through fronts of both sts and k2tog as usual.

Note: Afghan is worked from side to side.

INSTRUCTIONS

Cast on 274 sts. Do not join in round, but work back and forth on circular needle as follows:

Row 1: Knit.

Row 2: (*right side*) Purl.

Row 3: Knit.

Row 4: Purl.

Row 5: Knit.

Row 6: K2tog, *k8, yo, k2, yo, k8, SK2P; rep from * across, ending last rep with ssk instead of SK2P.

Row 7: Purl.

Rows 8-13: Repeat Rows 6 and 7 three times.

Now rep Rows 2-13 for pattern 27 times more, then Rows 2-4 once more (piece should measure approximately 48" [124.5 cm] at this point).

Cast off knitwise, being sure not to cast off too tight causing the edge to pucker, or too loose causing the edge to hang apart.

Tassels: Cut rem yarn into 8" [20.5 cm] lengths.

Group 5 lengths of yarn for each tassel.

Now using a large crochet hook, knot a tassel through ends of each ridge (formed by Rows 2-5), across both short ends of afghan. Trim ends to neaten.

Knit Basketweave Throw

EASY

SHOPPING LIST

Yarn (Worsted Weight) MEDIUM 4

Mary Maxim Starlette Ragg

[3.5 ounces, 210 yards

(100 grams, 192 meters) per ball]:

☐ Any Color 13 balls

Knitting Needle

36" (90 cm) Circular Needle

☐ Size 15 (10.00 mm)

or size needed for gauge

SIZE INFORMATION

Finished: 47.5" x 58.5"
[120.5 x 148.5 cm]

GAUGE INFORMATION

10 sts and 14 rows to 4" [10 cm], measured over pattern using 2 strands of yarn and **suggested** needle or any size needle which will give the correct stitch gauge.

STITCH GUIDE

Note: This entire afghan is worked using 2 strands of yarn held together throughout.

INSTRUCTIONS

To Make: Using 2 strands of yarn tog, cast on 108 sts loosely. Now working back and forth on circular needle, work in ribbing as follows:

Row 1: (*right side*) K3, *p2, k2; rep from * to last st, k1.

Row 2: K1, p2, *k2, p2; rep from * to last st, k1.

Repeat these 2 rows 4 times more - 10 rows in all.

Now work in Basketweave pattern as follows:

Rows 1, 3, 5 and 7: (*right side*) K 10, *p8, k8; rep from * to last 2 sts, k2.

Rows 2, 4, 6 and 8: K2, p8, *k8, p8; rep from * to last 2 sts, k2.

Rows 9, 11, 13 and 15: K2, p8, *k8, p8; rep from * to last 2 sts, k2.

Rows 10, 12, 14 and 16: K 10, *p8, k8; rep from * to last 2 sts, k2.

Repeat these 16 rows of pattern until piece measures approximately 55.5" [141 cm] from cast on edge, ending after a Row 8 or 16.

Next Row: K3, *p2, k2; rep from * to last st, k1.

Next Row: K1, p2, *k2, p2; rep from * to last st, k1.

Repeat these last 2 rows 4 times more.

Cast off loosely ribwise.

Side Borders: With right side of Throw facing, beg at bottom edge of ribbing, pick up and k8 sts evenly along side edge of ribbing, pick up and k 140 sts evenly along Basketweave section, pick up and k8 sts evenly along side edge of ribbing - 156 sts.

Now work ribbing as follows:

Row 1: K3, *p2, k2; rep from * to last st, k1.

Row 2: K1, p2, *k2, p2; rep from * to last st, k1.

Repeat these 2 rows 4 times more.

Cast off loosely ribwise.

Repeat for other side of Throw.

Dramatically Simple

INTERMEDIATE

SHOPPING LIST

Yarn (Worsted Weight) MEDIUM 4

Mary Maxim Starlette Ragg
[3.5 ounces, 210 yards
(100 grams, 192 meters) per ball]:

- ☐ Black or Blue (MC) 6 balls

Mary Maxim Starlette
[3.5 ounces, 180 yards
(100 grams, 165 meters) per ball]:

- ☐ Red or Yellow (CC 1) 4 balls
- ☐ Black or Blue (CC 2) 4 balls

Knitting Needle:

36" (90 cm) Circular Needle

- ☐ Size 9 (5.50 mm)

or size needed for gauge

SIZE INFORMATION

Finished: 47" x 60" [122 x 152.5 cm]

GAUGE INFORMATION

20 sts to 4" [10 cm] over pattern, using **suggested** needle or any size needle required to obtain the correct gauge or tension.

STITCH GUIDE

Notes:

This afghan is worked from side to side.

Stitches should not be counted after decrease row.

To avoid sewing in ends when afghan is completed, work them in as you go OR leave a 4" [10 cm] length of yarn at the beginning and end of each color change. These yarn tails can be incorporated as the fringe is made.

INSTRUCTIONS

Using circular needle and CC 1 yarn, cast on 300 sts.

Now working back and forth on circular needle, make Left Border as follows:

Row 1: (*wrong side, dec row*)
P1, *k2tog; rep from * to last st, p1 - 151 sts.

Row 2: K1, *knit into front and back of next st; rep from * to last st, k1 – 300 sts.

Row 3: Purl.

Change to MC yarn and work in pattern as follows:

Row 1: (*right side*) Knit.

Row 2: (*dec row*) P1, *k2tog; rep from * to last st, p1 - 151 sts.

Row 3: K1, *knit into front and back of next st; rep from * to last st, k1 - 300 sts.

Row 4: Purl.

These last four rows form the Striped Stitch Pattern.

Repeat these four rows throughout, changing colors as follows:

4 rows of CC 1, 4 rows of MC,
4 rows of CC 2, 4 rows of MC,
4 rows of CC 2, 4 rows of MC,
4 rows of CC 1.

Now rep these last 32 rows, 8 times more – 73 stripes (including the Left Border).

Work 4 rows of MC and finish the last stripe, Right Border, with these following 3 rows in CC 1;

Row 1: Knit.

Row 2: (*dec row*) P1, *k2tog; rep from * to last st, p1.

Row 3: K1, * knit into front and back of next st; rep from * to last st, k1.

Cast off knitwise.

Designed By: Mary Hobbs

TOP KNITTED EDGING:

Using CC 1, beg at the top right corner, pick up and k approximately 3 sts for every 4 rows across the top end of the stripes, taking care to end with an EVEN number of sts.

Row 1: (*dec row*) P1, *k2tog; rep from * to last st, p1.

Row 2: K1, * knit into front and back of next st; rep from * to last st, k1.

Cast off knitwise.

FRINGE:

Fringe is added to the lower edge of afghan, one tassel in the middle of each stripe. Each tassel corresponds with color of stripe.

To make the fringe, cut yarn into 8" [20.5 cm] lengths.

**Take 4 strands (only 3, if you have left tails) for a tassel and fold in half to make a loop, making sure ends are even. Insert a crochet hook through the edge of the afghan, in the middle of the stripe. Use hook to pull this loop through edge of afghan. Pull all the strands carefully through the loop (including the tails), tightening the knot evenly.

Repeat from ** across the lower edge of the afghan, trim to neaten.

An Alternate Color Combination

Perfect for the summer cottage or to brighten a dull day!

General Instructions

ABBREVIATIONS

"	inches
approx.	approximately
beg	begin or beginning
CC	Contrast Color
cm	centimeter
dec	decrease or decreasing
gm	gram
inc	increase or increasing
K	knit
kfb	knit into front & back of st
P	purl
PM	place marker
psso	pass slipped stitch over
M	marker
MC	Main Color
mm	milimeter
rem	remain or remaining
rep	repeat
rnd	round
sl	slip
st	stitch
sts	stitches
St st	Stocking stitch
tbl	through back loop
tog	together
yb	bring yarn to back of work
yds	yards
yf	bring yarn in front of work
yo	yarn over
yrn	yarn forward and around needle

SYMBOLS & TERMS

*** or #** work instructions following or between * or # as many more times as indicated in addition to the first time.

() or [ ] work enclosed instructions as many times as specified by the number immediately following **or** work all enclosed instructions in the stitch or space indicated **or** contains explanatory remarks

— the number(s) given after a hyphen at the end of a row or round denote(s) the number of stitches or spaces you should have on that row or round.

Yarn Weight Symbol & Names	1 SUPER FINE	2 FINE	3 LIGHT	4 MEDIUM	5 BULKY	6 SUPER BULKY	7 JUMBO
Type of Yarns in Category	Sock, Fingering Baby	Sport, Baby	DK, Light Worsted	Worsted, Afghan Aran	Chunky, Craft, Rug	Super Bulky, Roving	Jumbo, Roving
Knit Gauge Range in Stockinette St to 4" (10 cm)	27-32 sts	23-26 sts	21-24 sts	16-20 sts	12-15 sts	7-11 sts	6 sts and fewer
Advised Needle Size Range	1 to 3	3 to 5	5 to 7	7 to 9	9 to 11	11 to 17	17 and larger

*GUIDELINES ONLY: The chart above reflects the most commonly used gauges and needle sizes for specific yarn categories.

KNIT TERMINOLOGY		
UNITED STATES		INTERNATIONAL
gauge	=	tension
bind off	=	cast off

BEGINNER	Projects for first-time knitters using basic knit and purl stitches. Minimal shaping.
EASY	Projects using basic stitches, repetitve stitch patterns, simple color changes, and simple shaping and finishing.
INTERMEDIATE	Projects with a variety of stitches, such as basic cables and lace, simple intarsia, double-pointed needles and knitting in the round needle techniques, mid-level shaping and finishing.
EXPERIENCED	Projects using advanced techniques and stitches, such as short rows, fair isle, more intricate intarsia, cables, lace patterns and numerous color changes.

KNITTING NEEDLES

U.S.	50	35	19	17	15	13	11	----	----	10.5	10	9	8	7	6	5	4	3	----	2	1	0	----
U.K.	---	----	----	----	000	00	0	1	2	3	4	5	6	7	8	9	----	10	11	12	13	14	15
Metric mm	25	19	15	12.75	10	9	8	7.5	7	6.5	6	5.5	5	4.5	4	3.75	3.5	3.25	3	2.75	2.25	2	1.75

Casting On

1a 1b

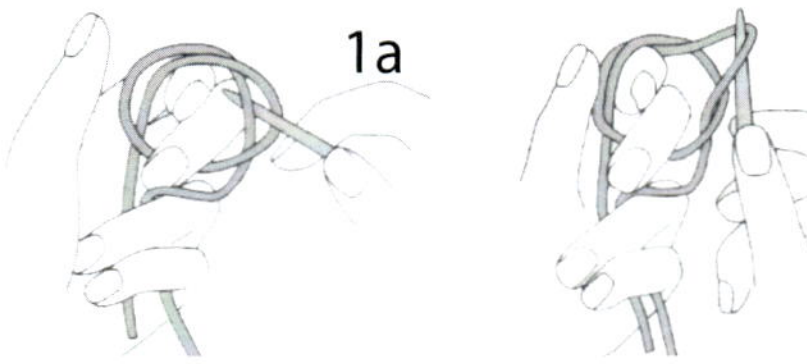

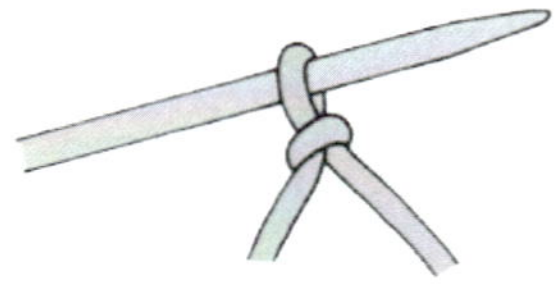

3a 3b

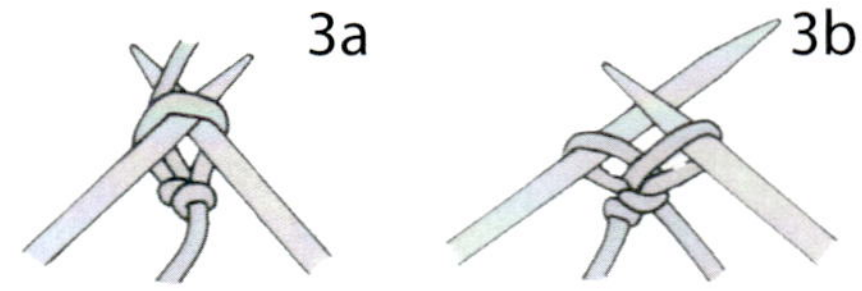

1a. Make a slip knot: Loop the yarn as shown and slip needle under the lower strand of the loop.
1b. Pull up a loop of yarn.

2. Pull the yarn end attached to the ball of yarn to tighten the slip knot leaving the other end approx. 4" [10 cm] long. Transfer needle to left hand.

3a. Insert the right-hand needle through slip knot and wind yarn over right-hand needle.
3b. Pull loop through slip knot.

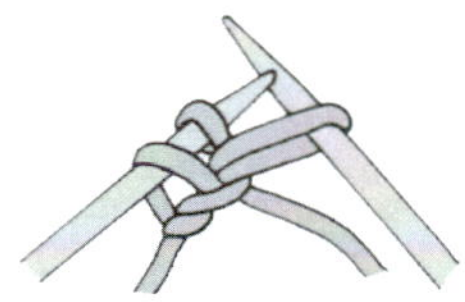

4. Place new loop on left-handle needle. (You now have 2 stitches (sts) on your left-hand needle.)

5. Insert right-hand needle between last 2 stitches (sts) on left-hand needle and wind yarn over right-hand needle.

6. Pull loop through. Place this new loop on left-hand needle beside last stitch (st). (You now have 1 more stitch on left-hand needle). Repeat (rep) steps 5 and 6 until required number of stitches (sts) have been cast on left-hand needle.

The Knit Stitch

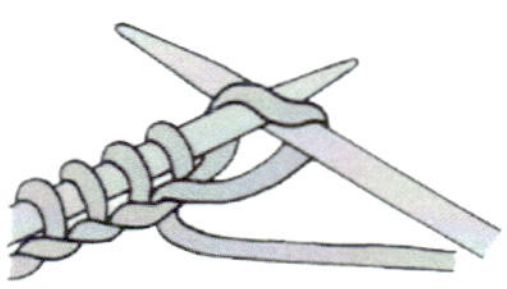

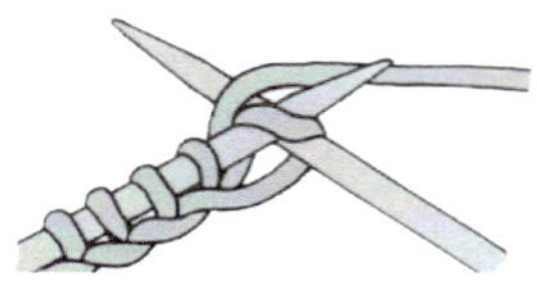

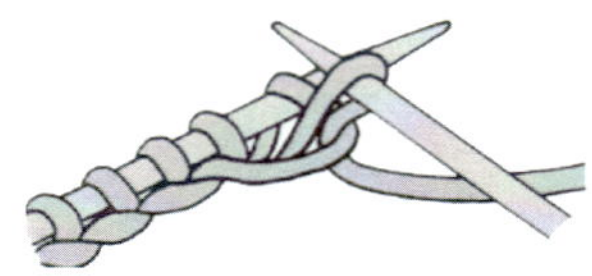

1. Hold the needle with cast on stitches (sts) in your left hand, and the loose yarn attached to the ball at the back of work. Insert right-hand needle from left to right through the front of the first stitch (st) on the left-hand needle.

2. Wind the yarn from left to right over the point of the right-hand needle.

3. Draw the yarn through this original stitch (st) which forms a new stitch (st) on right-hand needle.

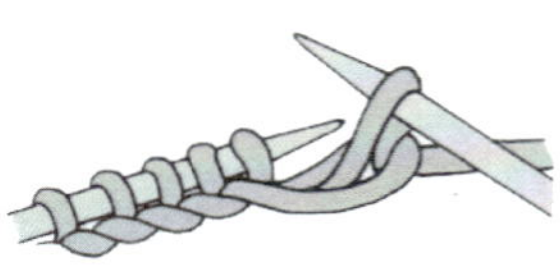

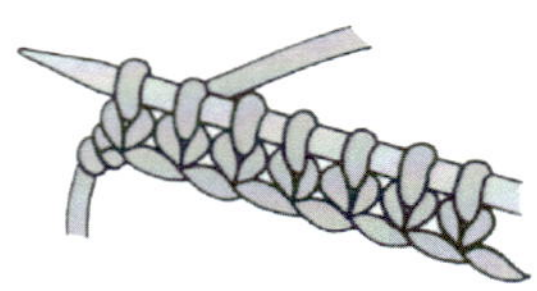

4. Slip the original stitch (st) off the left-hand needle, keeping the new stitch (st) on the right-hand needle.

5. To knit a row, repeat steps 1 to 4 until all stitches (sts) have been transferred from left-hand needle to right-hand needle. Turn the work by transferring the needle with stitches (sts) into your left hand to knit the next row.

The Purl Stitch

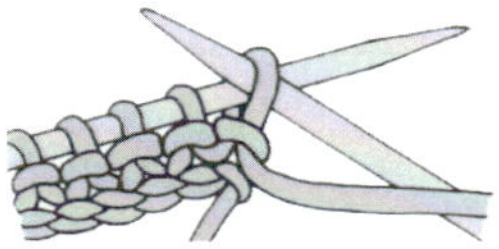

1. With yarn at front of work, insert right-hand needle from right to left through front of first stitch (st) on left-hand needle.

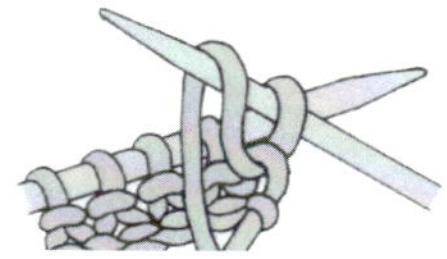

2. Wind yarn around right-hand needle. Pull yarn through stitch (st).

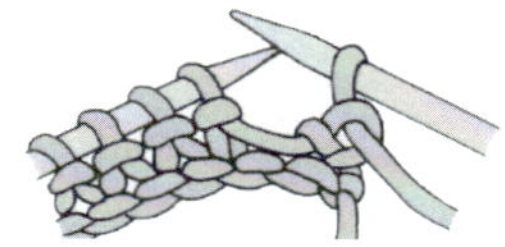

3. Slip original stitch (st) off needle. Repeat (rep) these steps until all stitches (sts) on left-hand needle have been transferred onto right-hand needle to complete one row of purling.

Increasing and Decreasing

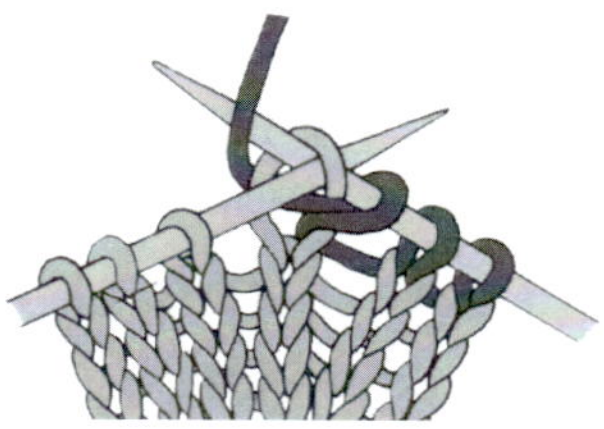

Increase 1 stitch (st) in next stitch (st): Work into front and back of stitch (st) as follows: Knit stitch (st), then before slipping it off needle, twist right-hand needle behind left-hand needle and knit again into back of loop. Slip original stitch (st) off needle. There are now 2 stitches (sts) on right-hand needle made from original stitch.

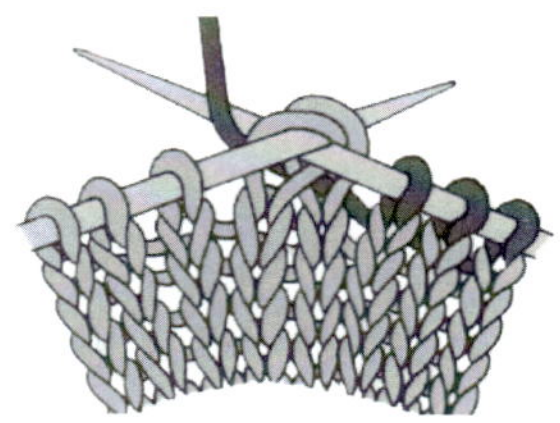

K2tog Decrease: Knit 2 stitches (sts) together (tog) through the front of both loops.

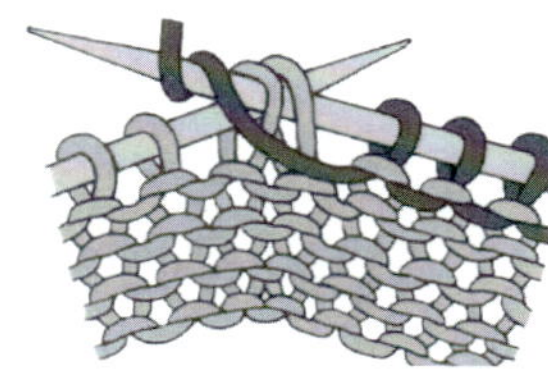

P2tog Decrease: Purl 2 stitches (sts) together (tog) through the front of both loops.

Casting Off

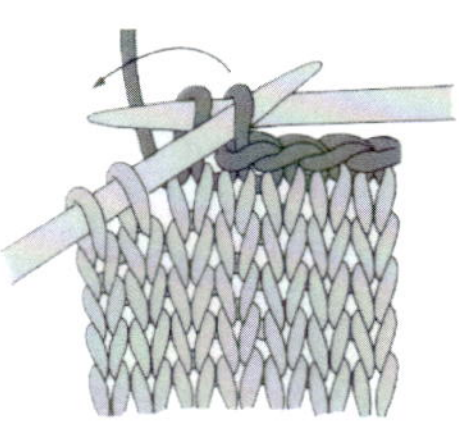

Cast off using knit stitch (knitwise): Knit the first 2 stitches (sts). *Using left-hand needle, lift first stitch (st) over second stitch (st) and drop it off between points of the 2 needles. Knit the next stitch (st); repeat (rep) from * until all stitches (sts) from left-hand needle have been worked and only 1 stitch (st) remains on the right-hand needle. Cut yarn (leaving enough to sew in end) and thread cut end through stitch (st) on needle. Draw yarn up firmly to fasten off last stitch (st).

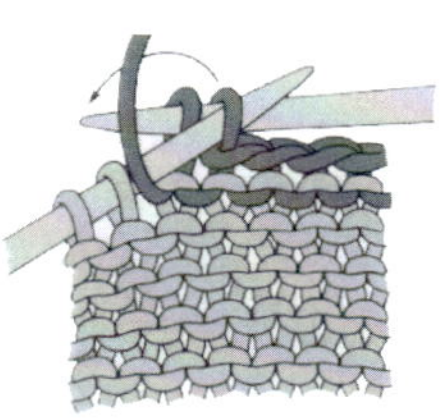

Cast off using purl stitch (purlwise): Purl first 2 stitches (sts). *Using left-hand needle, lift first stitch (st) over second stitch (st) and drop it off needle. Purl next stitch (st) as described for casting off knitwise.

Yarn Information

Projects in this book were made with different weight yarns. Any brand of yarn may be used. It is best to refer to yardage/meters when determining how many balls or skeins to purchase. Remember, to arrive at the finished size, it is the GAUGE/TENSION that is important, not the brand of yarn. For your convenience, listed below are the specific yarn ranges used to create our photographed models.

Cozy Colorful Throw
Mary Maxim's Prism

Uptown Throw
Mary Maxim's Studio

Cables & Twists Throw
Mary Maxim's Woodlands

Dreams of Ireland
Mary Maxim's Aran Irish Twist

Lilies & Lace Throw
Mary Maxim's Ultra Mellowspun

Crimson Comfort
Mary Maxim's Best Value

Paneled Lace Throw
Mary Maxim's Milan

Vertical Zigzag Throw
Mary Maxim's Starlette

Knit Basketweave Throw
Mary Maxim's Starlette Ragg

Dramatically Simple
Mary Maxim's Starlette Ragg
Mary Maxim's Starlette

Made in U.S.A.